CURIOUS
ABOUT
ICE CREAM

by Bonnie Bader

PENGUIN YOUNG READERS LICENSES

An Imprint of Penguin Random House

PENGUIN YOUNG READERS LICENSES

An Imprint of Penguin Random House LLC

Smithsonian

This trademark is owned by the Smithsonian Institution and
is registered in the U.S. Patent and Trademark Office.

Smithsonian Enterprises:
Christopher Liedel, President
Carol LeBlanc, Senior Vice President, Education and Consumer Products
Brigid Ferraro, Vice President, Education and Consumer Products
Ellen Nanney, Licensing Manager
Kealy Gordon, Product Development Manager

Smithsonian National Museum of American History, Kenneth E. Behring Center:
Jessica Carbone, Project Associate for the American Food and Wine History Project

PHOTO CREDITS: front cover (top to bottom): (blue-green, purple, and nut ice cream bars): jenifoto/iStock/Thinkstock, (purple ice cream cone): alisafarov/iStock/Thinkstock, (chocolate, orange, pink, twirly, and yellow-green ice cream bars): photka/iStock/Thinkstock, (soft serve): carlosbezz/iStock/Thinkstock, (orange soda): bhofack2/iStock/Thinkstock, (sundae): Jupiterimages/Stockbyte/Thinkstock, (dark pink cone and three-scoops ice cream cone): unpict/iStock/Thinkstock; back cover (top left to bottom right): (root beer float): Biogeek/iStock/Thinkstock, (drumstick ice cream and watermelon bar): photka/iStock/Thinkstock, (sundae): mvp64/iStock/Thinkstock; page 1: (dark pink cone and three-scoops ice cream cone): unpict/iStock/Thinkstock, (blue-green ice cream bar): jenifoto/iStock/Thinkstock, (chocolate, orange, twirly, and yellow-green ice cream bars): photka/iStock/Thinkstock; page 2 (top to bottom): (drumstick ice cream and watermelon bar): photka/iStock/Thinkstock, (purple ice cream cone): alisafarov/iStock/Thinkstock, (purple ice cream bar): jenifoto/iStock/Thinkstock; page 3, page 6 (bottom), pages 8–9 (center), page 11, page 17 (right): Smithsonian National Museum of American History; page 4: (evergreen): martateron/iStock/Thinkstock, (honey): Volosina/iStock/Thinkstock, (Alexander the Great): Photos.com/Thinkstock; page 5: Photos.com/Thinkstock; page 6: (George Washington): GeorgiosArt/iStock/Thinkstock; page 7: (ice cream cooler): Cooper Hewitt, Smithsonian Design Museum; (Thomas Jefferson): Wynnter/iStock/Thinkstock; page 7 (right), page 8 (right), page 12, page 13, page 16 (top right, bottom left), page 19, page 24, page 26, page 27 (top left, right), page 28, page 30 (bottom left): Library of Congress; page 9: (top): karanaev/iStock/Thinkstock, (bottom): Handmade Pictures/iStock/Thinkstock; page 10: United States Patent and Trademark Office; page 14: Porterhse/Wikimedia Commons (CC0 1.0); page 15: (left) unpict/iStock/Thinkstock, (right) chas53/iStock/Thinkstock; page 16 (top left): photka/iStock/Thinkstock; page 17 (left): unpict/iStock/Thinkstock; page 18: (top): National Archives, (bottom): JoyTasa/iStock/Thinkstock; pages 20–21: Carvel; pages 22–23: Dairy Queen; page 25: Tichnor Brothers Postcard Collection/Boston Public Library/Digital Commonwealth; page 27 (bottom left): foodandstyle/iStock/Thinkstock; page 29: U.S. Naval Institute; page 30: (top right): Häagen-Dazs, (sundae): mvp64/iStock/Thinkstock; page 31: (top): NASA, (bottom): unpict/iStock/Thinkstock; page 32 (top to bottom): (purple and nut ice cream bars): jenifoto/iStock/Thinkstock, (dark pink cone and three-scoops ice cream cone): unpict/iStock/Thinkstock, (orange ice cream bar): photka/iStock/Thinkstock, (purple ice cream cone): alisafarov/iStock/Thinkstock, (orange soda): bhofack2/iStock/Thinkstock.

ISBN 9780515157734

10 9 8 7 6 5 4 3 2 1

"I scream. You scream. We all scream for ICE CREAM!"

People really, really love ice cream. Nine out of ten Americans eat ice cream. And they each eat about twenty-two pounds of it every year. That's a lot of ice cream!

Where did this cold, sweet, creamy treat come from?

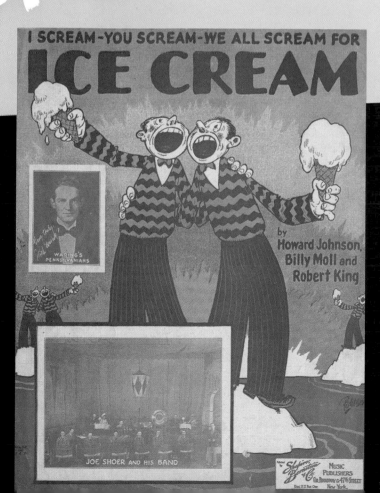

No one knows exactly who invented ice cream.

More than two thousand years ago, Alexander the Great, a king of ancient Greece, enjoyed eating snow and ice flavored with honey and **nectar**.

Alexander the Great

Emperors in China also ate something like ice cream over a thousand years ago. It was made with heated milk, flour, and oil from an evergreen tree. The mixture was poured into metal tubes, which were then placed in ice. Once frozen, it was ready to eat!

Marco Polo

Explorer Marco Polo visited the Far East from around 1270 to 1290. Stories say he returned to Italy with a recipe for a cold treat similar to **sherbet**.

Rich **colonists** from Europe most likely brought the recipe for ice cream to America in the 1700s.

The first president of the United States liked ice cream. George Washington had his own device he called a "cream machine for ice." He also owned an ice cream serving spoon.

George Washington

An ice cream mold that shows George Washington

Thomas Jefferson

Thomas Jefferson's ice cream recipe

41868

This ice cream cooler would be used as a serving dish.

President Thomas Jefferson loved ice cream, too. He even had his own recipe for making it!

Although ice cream was a favorite dessert of some US presidents, a former slave known as Aunt Sallie Shadd helped put ice cream on the White House menu. Shadd owned a **catering** business in Wilmington, Delaware. She became famous for a dessert she made from frozen cream, sugar, and fruit.

Dolley Madison, the wife of President James Madison, loved the sweet treat. She made it the official dessert of White House dinners.

Dolley Madison

Dolley Madison dinner plate

In the 1820s, White House cook Augustus Jackson mixed salt with ice in his dessert. This helped lower and control the temperature of the **ingredients**. Some people called Jackson the "father of ice cream." That's because he made it so much easier to create the cold treat. He later sold his new and improved ice cream in tin cans to street **vendors** and ice cream parlors in Philadelphia.

Soon you could make and eat ice cream at home. Nancy M. Johnson invented the hand-cranked ice cream freezer in 1843. It had a large wooden bucket with a smaller tin can inside.

N. M. JOHNSON.
ARTIFICIAL FREEZER.

No. 3,254.

Patented Sept. 9, 1843.

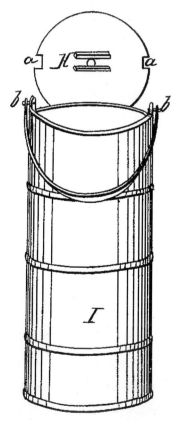

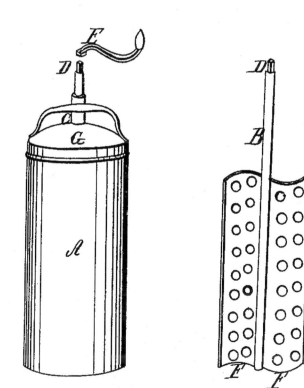

Nancy Johnson's plans

You filled the space in between them with ice and rock salt. Next you poured heavy cream into the inner can and bolted on the lid. Then, you

cranked,

cranked,

cranked

the handle until the mixture froze and became *ice* cream!

An ice cream freezer from 1910

Ice cream ingredients were expensive. For a long time, people mostly ate it on special occasions. Selling ice cream wasn't much of a business until Jacob Fussell came along.

Fussell was a businessman who sold milk and cream from farmers in Baltimore, Maryland. But he couldn't always sell everything he had. So he put the leftovers to good use and produced ice cream! Fussell built an ice cream factory in Seven Valleys, Pennsylvania, in 1852. He packed his ice cream in ice, put it on trains, and shipped it to Baltimore. His business was a huge success!

Many ice cream vendors were **immigrants** from Italy. They may have called out words that sounded like "hokey-pokey."

Ice cream was sold by these "Hokey-Pokey" vendors who pushed ice cream carts on the street. The first Hokey-Pokey men started selling in 1828. By 1901 there were over 4,000 Hokey-Pokey vendors rolling along the New York City streets. Some of them were women and girls. On hot summer days, they were surrounded by kids!

Eating a dish of ice cream was great, but eating an ice cream sundae was even better!

Some people say this dessert was invented in Two Rivers, Wisconsin, in 1881. An owner of a soda fountain shop there spooned a bit of chocolate sauce over ice cream for a customer. Delicious!

ICE CREAM SUNDAE

In 1881, George Hallauer asked Edward C. Berner, the owner of a soda fountain at 1404-15th Street, to top a dish of ice cream with chocolate sauce, hitherto used only for ice cream sodas. The concoction cost a nickel and soon became very popular, but was sold only on Sundays.

One day a ten year old girl insisted she have a dish of ice cream "with that stuff on top," saying they could "pretend it was Sunday." After that, the confection was sold every day in many flavors. It lost its Sunday-only association, to be called ICE CREAM SUNDAE when a glassware salesman placed an order with his company for the long canoe-shaped dishes in which it was served, as "sundae dishes."

Erected 1973

Others say the sundae was invented in a soda fountain shop in Ithaca, New York. There a local priest was served vanilla ice cream covered in cherry syrup with a candied cherry on top. The priest suggested that the dessert be named after the day, which was Sunday.

Whether it was a scoop or a sundae, ice cream was served in a dish. That changed around the 1900s. Ice cream cones were invented!

Italo Marchiony, an Italian immigrant, baked dough in little cups with handles. He filled each cup with ice cream. You could eat the whole thing.

Another vendor sold ice cream at the World's Fair in St. Louis, Missouri, in 1904. He ran out of cardboard serving dishes. At a booth nearby, Ernest A. Hamwi was trying to sell waffles. No one was buying them because it was too hot outside. Hamwi rolled up his waffles into cones to help out the ice cream vendor.

Eating cones at the St. Louis World's Fair

How do you keep ice cream cold? Put it in the icebox . . . if you have one!

In the early 1900s, not many people had refrigerators, which were also known as iceboxes. The first home refrigerator appeared in 1911. As refrigerators with built-in freezers became more popular, so did ice cream.

In 1899, 5 million gallons of ice cream were made each year in the United States. By 1919, 150 million gallons were being made!

FUN FACT

It takes 12 gallons of milk to create one gallon of ice cream. Over her entire lifetime, a cow can produce enough milk for 9,000 gallons of ice cream.

In 1920, a **confectioner** named Harry Burt covered vanilla ice cream with a hard chocolate coating. His daughter tried it out. Tasty! But too messy to eat with your hands.

Burt's son suggested putting sticks in the treat.
The Good Humor Bar was born.

Harry Burt bought twelve trucks, built freezers inside, and added bells. People would know when his ice cream trucks were coming down the street.

HUCKLEBERRY FINN GOOD HUMOR

Good Humor

ICE CREAM

30

Washington, DC, 1944

Sometimes, melted ice cream isn't so bad.

On a hot summer day in Hartsdale, New York, in 1934, Tom Carvel's ice cream truck got a flat tire. His ice cream started to melt! People passing by bought it anyway, and no one complained. In fact, they loved it! Tom sold "soft serve" ice cream for the rest of the summer. He earned about $3,500, which is about $60,000 today!

In 1936, Tom opened his first Carvel ice cream store—right where his truck had broken down!

J.F. "Grandpa" McCullough

Carvel soon had competition. In 1938, J.F. "Grandpa" McCullough and his son Alex McCullough opened up Dairy Queen in Joliet, Illinois. Grandpa knew the ice cream mix tasted best before it was frozen to its final form. That's because really cold ice cream numbs your taste buds.

The McCulloughs introduced their type of ice cream with a sale: "all the ice cream you can eat for 10 cents." They dished up 1,600 servings in two hours.

While soft ice cream was being swirled out into cones and cups, ice cream was also being sold in soda.

Several people claim they invented the ice-cream soda. The most popular story is about Robert M. Green of Philadelphia. In 1874, he was selling a popular drink made from sweet cream, syrup, and soda water. One day, Green ran out of cream, so he scooped in ice cream instead. People loved it.

Through the 1950s, ice-cream sodas were served up at counters manned by soda jerks. They were called this because they had to jerk the arm of the soda fountain to make the soda water flow. Many teenagers worked this popular job.

On a farm, 1935

In the 1930s and 1940s, ice cream was being made, sold, and eaten all over America!

Ice cream week at the White House, 1937

NATIONAL ICE CREAM WEEK
APRIL 18 TO 24

St. Augustine, Texas, 1939

Making ice cream, 1940

Ice cream was a delicious treat, but it was also given as a reward. During World War II, when a ship's crew rescued an American pilot, they got twenty gallons of ice cream.

In 1945, the United States Navy built a floating ice cream parlor for sailors. Every hour about 5,400 gallons of ice cream were made on board this **barge**!

In the 1960s and 1970s, a lot of new ice cream companies popped up.

Reuben Mattus, a Polish immigrant who lived in the Bronx, New York, started Häagen-Dazs in 1960 with three simple ice cream flavors: vanilla, chocolate, and coffee.

In 1978, Ben Cohen and Jerry Greenfield took a five-dollar correspondence course in how to make ice cream. Ben and Jerry opened their first ice cream shop in a renovated gas station in Burlington, Vermont.

In 1984, President Ronald Reagan declared July to be National Ice Cream Month.

Lots of people think ice cream
is out of this world—especially astronauts.
At first, they ate crumbly freeze-dried
ice cream. Then, in 2006, cold, creamy ice
cream was packed into a freezer aboard
Space Shuttle Atlantis. Now astronauts on
the International Space Station can grab a
cup of frozen ice cream.

I scream, you scream—wherever you are,
you can always scream for ice cream!

FUN FACT

The most popular
ice cream flavor in the
US is vanilla, followed
by chocolate and
strawberry.

GLOSSARY

barge: a flat-bottom boat used for carrying heavy loads

catering: cooking and serving food

colonists: people who live in places that are ruled by another country

confectioner: a person who sells chocolate and other candy

correspondence: writing letters back and forth

emperors: rulers with great power

immigrants: people who leave one country to go live in another country

ingredients: items that are used to make something

nectar: a thick juice made from fruit

sherbet: a frozen, fruit-flavored dessert

vendors: people who sell something